MORIARTY

THE STARS

Contents

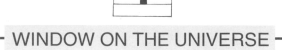

WINDOW ON THE UNIVERSE

THE STARS

Barron's Educational Series

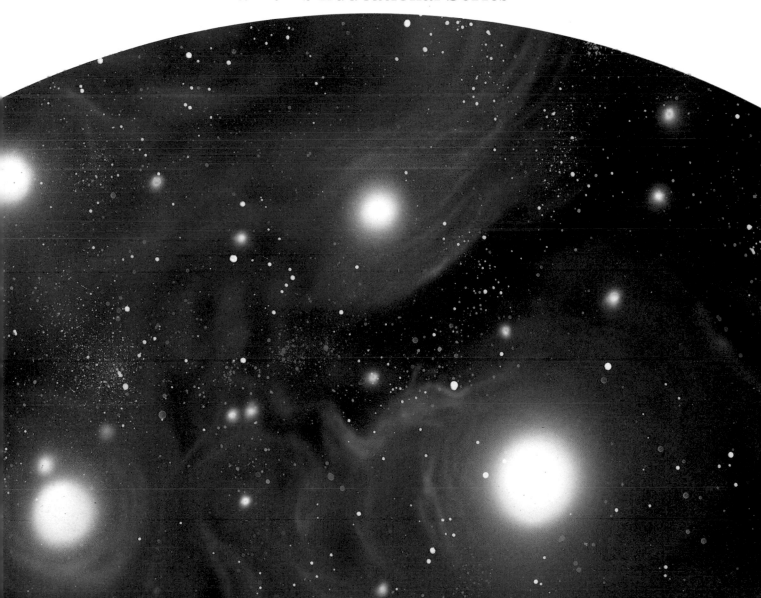

The distance to the stars

At night the stars simply appear as points of light in the sky. There are all kinds; some are very bright and others are faint. The brightest are of magnitude designations that are less than zero. The faintest ones that can be seen with the naked eye are of magnitude six.

In our daily life, we can tell how far away the objects we see are because we have two eyes. Because our eyes are slightly separated, each one sees a slightly different image. Try stretching your arm out and looking at your raised thumb, first closing one eye, and then the other. You will see how the position of your thumb in relation to the background appears differently to each eye.

With the stars, we can do something similar. If we take advantage of the Earth's movement around the Sun and observe the stars six months apart, we can measure how the positions of the closest stars change slightly in relation to the ones that are farthest away. This change allows us to calculate their distances from the Earth. It turns out that the closest stars are so far away that their light takes about four years to reach us. We say that they are about four **light years** away. Most of the stars we see at night are much further away, tens or hundreds of light years away.

What would the Sun look like if it were as far away as other stars, for example, 30 light years away? It would be a fifth-magnitude star, barely visible in the sky to the naked eye. The only difference between the stars and the Sun is that we are much closer to the Sun so it looks brighter to us.

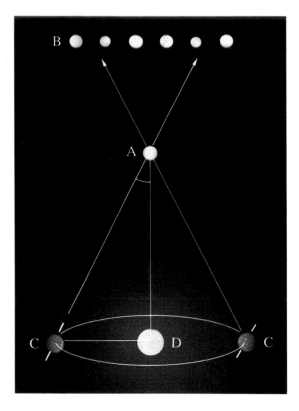

Left: We can determine the distance to a closer star (A) by observing its apparent position relative to the most distant stars (B), and comparing it to its apparent position six months later. Earth's two positions (C) are 180 million miles (300 million km) apart, twice the distance between Earth and the Sun (D). The different positions of the Earth let us see a slight difference in the position of the nearby stars.

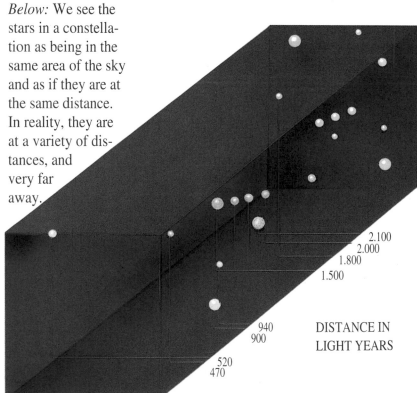

Below: We see the stars in a constellation as being in the same area of the sky and as if they are at the same distance. In reality, they are at a variety of distances, and very far away.

2.100
2.000
1.800
1.500

940
900

DISTANCE IN LIGHT YEARS

520
470

Below: The Orion nebula is a luminous cloud of interstellar gas, illuminated by young stars inside it. New stars are being born now in that cloud. The great nebula in Orion can be seen with the naked eye in the constellation of the same name. It is one of the most beautiful in the sky. Four very bright stars represent the shoulders and knees of Orion, the mythological giant. Three bright stars in a line form Orion's belt. A sword hangs from his belt, and in the middle of it the Orion nebula can be seen as a somewhat blurry object.

The color of the stars

Have you ever noticed the color of the stars? The light they put out varies somewhat in color from one star to another. In some cases you can see this difference easily. For example, in the constellation Orion, which is visible in the evening around December, the two brightest stars have distinct colors: Betelgeuse, in the northeast corner, is red; while Rigel, in the southwest corner, emits a blue-white light. The stars have a whole range of colors, from red to orange, yellow, white, and finally blue-white.

These color differences tell us how hot the star is. Every warm body emits light and heat (these are two possible forms of electromagnetic radiation), whether it is a star or an incandescent lightbulb. A lightbulb filament, heated by electric current, emits radiation, a small part of which is visible light. If, for example, the voltage drops, the temperature of the filament goes down and the light it emits turns yellowish or even reddish. If, on the other hand, the temperature of the filament rises, the light is not only more intense but also whiter and more bluish. The color of the light

emitted lets us know the temperature of the body that is emitting it.

In this way, we know that the material the stars are made of is so hot that it takes the form of a gas: stars are huge balls of gas, mostly hydrogen. This gas is extremely hot, and because of its high temperature it emits light and heat. The color of the light tells us the temperature of the star's surface.

Right: This illustration shows the temperature of the surfaces of the stars, according to their color. The hottest stars are bluish and have a surface temperature of about 55,000 degrees Fahrenheit. The Sun, a yellow star, has a surface temperature of about 11,000 degrees Fahrenheit. Red stars are the coolest, at only about 5,500 degrees.

Right: The color of the light emitted by a body depends on its temperature. If the filament of a lightbulb is not very hot, the light is reddish, while when the filament is very hot, the light is whiter.

55,000°F

36,000°F

18,000°F

14,500°F

11,000°F

7,500°F

5,500°F

Below: This illustration shows what appear to be trails left by the stars if viewed at various times because of the Earth's rotation. The whole sky appears to rotate in a direction opposite to the Earth, so that we see the stars trace circles around the pole. The thickest traces correspond to the brightest stars, while the more delicate ones are made by fainter stars. So it is easy to distinguish the different colors left by the stars' trails. The bluish trails are from very hot stars, while the reddish ones are from relatively cool stars.

Why do the stars shine?

The stars shine because they are hot. But where does a star get its energy to be hot? Until fairly recently, the answer to this question was unknown. It was Albert Einstein, developer of the theory of relativity at the beginning of this century, who answered this question: a small quantity of matter can be transformed into a large quantity of energy.

The stars are mostly made up of hydrogen. Hydrogen is the simplest natural element and the most common one in the universe. A hydrogen atom consists of a nucleus with a single proton and an electron.

The matter at the center of the star is very compressed by the weight of the star itself. This causes the protons that form the nuclei of the hydrogen atoms to collide violently with each other. As a result of these collisions, four hydrogen nuclei can come together to form a nucleus of helium. The helium nucleus is made up of two protons and two neutrons. During this process of **fusion**, two protons are transformed into neutrons,

emitting a positron (a light particle like an electron, but with a positive charge). The helium nucleus weights slightly less than the four hydrogen nuclei that formed it. This small quantity of matter that has disappeared releases a large quantity of energy.

Below: The nucleus of most stars is a true nuclear reactor, where fusion reactions take place. The hydrogen nuclei collide violently with each other. Four protons can merge and create a helium nucleus with two protons and two neutrons.

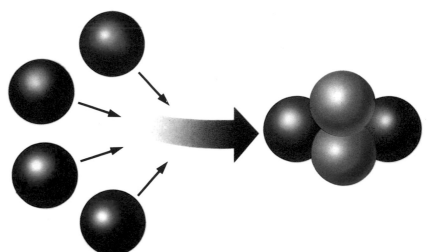

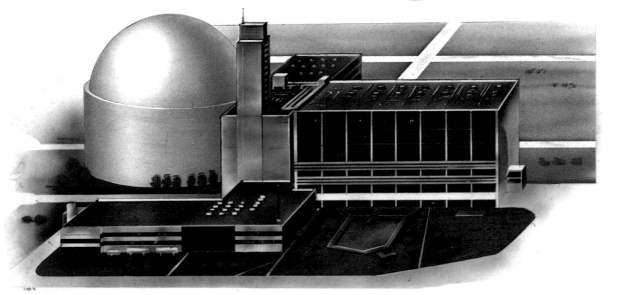

Left: Like a star, a nuclear power station gets its energy from nuclear reactions. But instead of getting it from the fusion of light nuclei, the power station gets energy from fission—the splitting—of heavy nuclei.

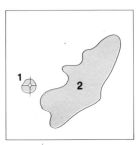

Below: The supernova 1987A ① suddenly appeared on February 24, 1987, in the Great Magellanic Cloud ② in the southern hemisphere. In this galaxy, which is close to ours, an old star had burst in an immense explosion. What had before been an ordinary star was transformed in a matter of hours into the most brilliant one in that part of the sky. Some stars end their lives this way, with a huge supernova explosion. Other stars also die, but in less spectacular ways.

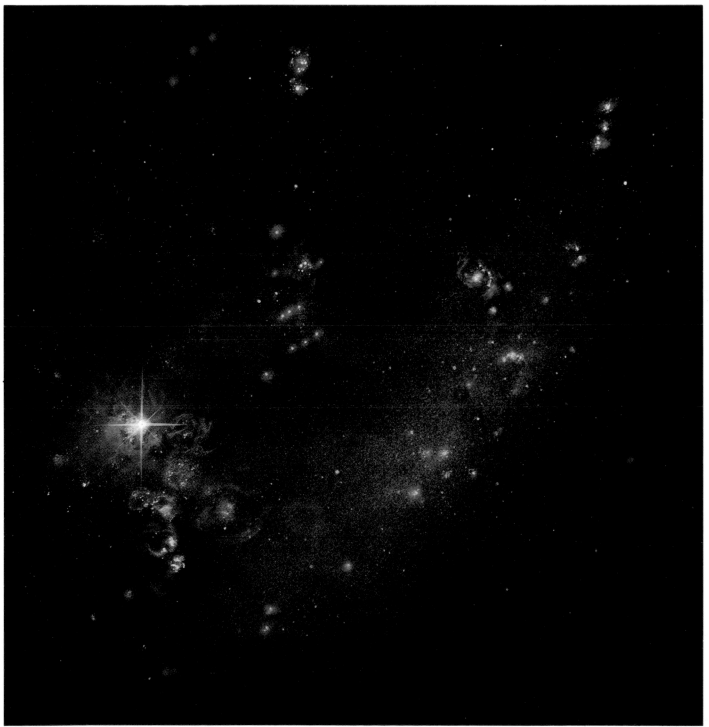

Groups of stars

The great majority of stars are not isolated, but rather form systems of two, or sometimes more, stars that are near each other in space. In these double systems, the stars revolve around each other because of the gravitational force between them. Milzar and Alcor, in Ursa Major, are a good example that can be seen with the naked eye.

Other groups of stars, called **star clusters**, contain hundreds or even thousands of stars. These are groups of stars that were formed simultaneously in the same part of the galaxy. One of the most beautiful star clusters is the one known as the Pleiades. Six stars that form a small dipper shape can be seen with the naked eye in the constellation Taurus. With some binoculars small groups of stars can be distinguished, and with a telescope hundreds of stars can be seen in the cluster. These stars are blue and luminous, all of the same age, and were formed recently from the same cloud of interstellar matter.

Some clusters that can be seen in the sky are extremely crowded. They have a spherical shape, and contain many, many stars. These are called **globular clusters.** There are many globular clusters near the constellation Sagittarius, which marks the center of our galaxy.

Left: The globular cluster in the constellation Hercules is made up of more than a million stars crowded together. The stars in this cluster are among the oldest in our galaxy.

Below: In Ursa Major, Mizar and Alcor (in the box) are visible with the naked eye. With a telescope, though, you can see (as shown in the enlarged box) that Mizar is a system made up of two stars.

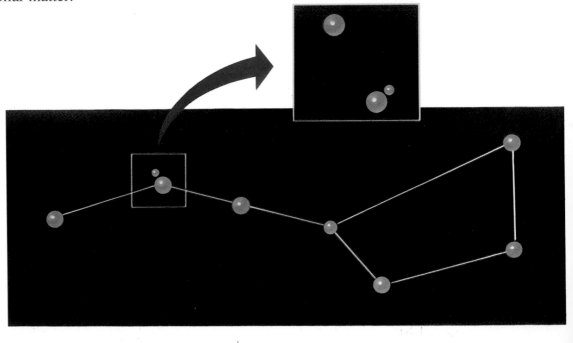

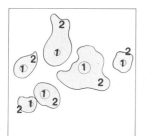

Below: The Pleiades are a group of young blue stars in the constellation Taurus. The cluster is made up of hundreds of stars, the brightest of which can be seen with the naked eye. Each of these stars ① is surrounded by a halo of gas and dust ② left over from the interstellar matter from which they were formed. The cloudiness around these stars will disperse completely when the stars are older.

The birth of the stars

We know that stars must have been formed at some time in the past. What were they formed from? The only reasonable answer is from existing gas and dust among the stars in the galaxy. This is called **interstellar matter**.

Under normal conditions, interstellar matter is not visible, but when illuminated by a hot, luminous star, it forms **bright nebulas** that have a rosy color.

The force governing this whole process of formation and, in fact, the star's subsequent life, is gravity. According to one theory, when a cloud of interstellar matter crosses a spiral arm of the galaxy, it begins to condense and the internal gravitational force increases. This makes the cloud contract more rapidly.

As the matter condenses, it breaks into pieces and gets hotter. The center of any very large piece reaches temperatures over a million degrees, giving rise to a **protostar**. Because of this high temperature, a reaction starts among the hydrogen nuclei. The energy produced at the center of the protostar stops the contraction and a new star has been formed.

The remnants of the initial cloud form a flat disc that revolves around the star. This matter can end up condensing and forming the planets that accompany the newly formed star.

Left: When a cloud of interstellar matter contracts enough, a very hot protostar is formed in the middle of it.

Below: The Orion Nebula, an area where many stars are being formed, is in the lower half of the constellation Orion.

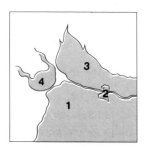

Below: Stars are formed by the gravitational contraction of a cloud of interstellar dust and gas. A **dark nebula** ① composed of interstellar dust hides the stars behind it. The Horsehead Nebula ② protrudes from this dark nebula behind a bright nebula ③. The brightest star ④ is Zeta Orionis, the star on the left in Orion's belt. The Horsehead nebula is a region in our galaxy where new stars are being formed even today.

Fully developed stars

A star, once it forms and begins to shine, is a stable body that remains practically unchanged for many years.

In the nucleus of the star, near its center, hydrogen is being converted into helium. The energy produced makes the interior of the star extraordinarily hot. This energy escapes from the surface of the star in the form of light and heat.

The gas formed by the star tends to expand, and is capable of supporting the weight of the star itself, stopping its contraction.

This situation lasts as long as there is enough hydrogen in the center of the star. When the hydrogen is exhausted, the star stops being a fully developed star and becomes an old star.

How long will it take the Sun to experience these changes and extinguish itself? If we take into account the amount of hydrogen in the Sun, and the pace at which it is being used up, we can tell that the Sun has enough hydrogen to shine for about 10 billion years after it formed. So the Sun is a middle-aged star. It formed about 5 billion years ago and it will continue to shine as brightly for 5 billion more years.

By contrast, the lives of other stars are much shorter. Their lifespans depend on their mass, that is, on the amount of matter in the star. The greater the amount of matter from which the star formed, the more condensed and hot its nucleus is. The star is brighter and hotter; its surface is bluish. A blue star uses up its hydrogen in only some millions of years, a very short time compared to the Sun. This is why we know that bright, blue stars like the Pleiades are young.

Below: Fully developed stars with a large mass are very bright and hot. They have a bluish color and use up hydrogen more rapidly than the Sun. Stars that are smaller than the Sun are reddish and use up hydrogen much more slowly. The illustration shows the sizes of these stars relative to the Sun, located at the upper right.

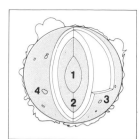

Below: In a fully developed star like the Sun, energy is produced in the extremely hot nucleus ①, where hydrogen is being transformed into helium. In the intermediate area ② energy is transported to the surface ③, which is not as hot as the star's center. The surface can have dark, colder spots ④.

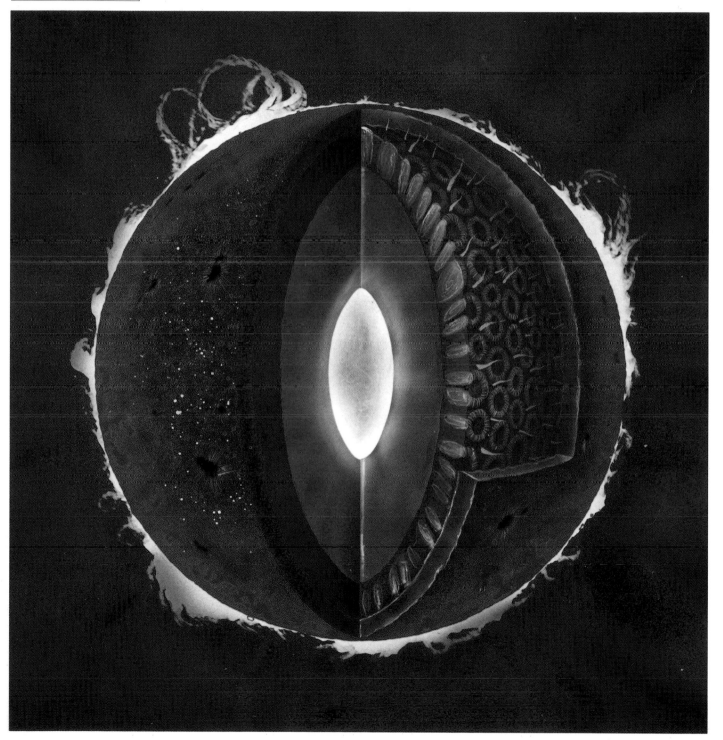

Giant stars

Stars finish their fully developed life when they have consumed all the hydrogen in their center. This happens when they have used up all their energy supply, which up to this point maintains the star's stability. The star's nucleus can no longer resist the rest of the star's weight, and begins to contract. Such compression makes the temperature of the nucleus rise and causes nuclear reactions in the layer surrounding the nucleus. The energy produced outside the center of the star makes the star's different layers dilate and cool. The star swells and then becomes reddish. This is what we call a **red giant**.

A typical red giant star is about one hundred times bigger than our Sun. When the Sun becomes a red star, in about 5 billion years, it will grow so big that it will reach and burn up the nearest planets, Mercury, Venus, and probably Earth.

Many stars in the red giant stage undergo periodic changes in brightness. This is because they expand and shrink rhythmically. They are called **pulsating variables.**

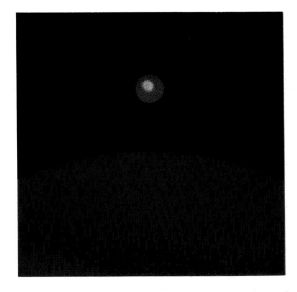

Left: A red giant has a very hot and compressed nucleus and a wrapping that is very cold and expanding. A typical red giant is one hundred times bigger than the Sun.

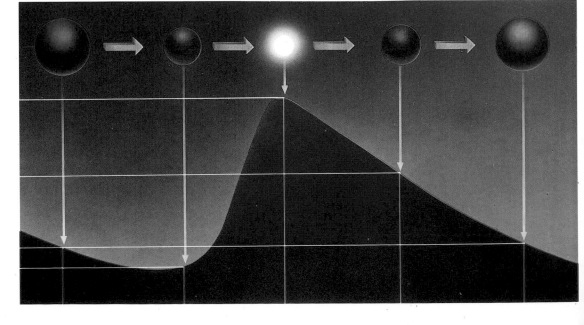

Right: Many red giants vary in brightness as shown in this graph. Stars are unstable. They dilate and cool down only to contract and heat up again.

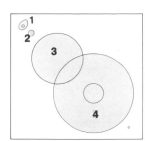

Below: Here we can see the evolution of the Sun. Like other stars, the Sun's life began from a cloud of interstellar matter ①. During its fully developed life, it produces energy by converting hydrogen into helium in its nucleus ②. This is the current stage, which will last for about 10 billion years. When it has used up all the hydrogen in its nucleus, the Sun will swell and become a red giant ③. Later on, the Sun will release a gas bubble ④ that will then become a white dwarf.

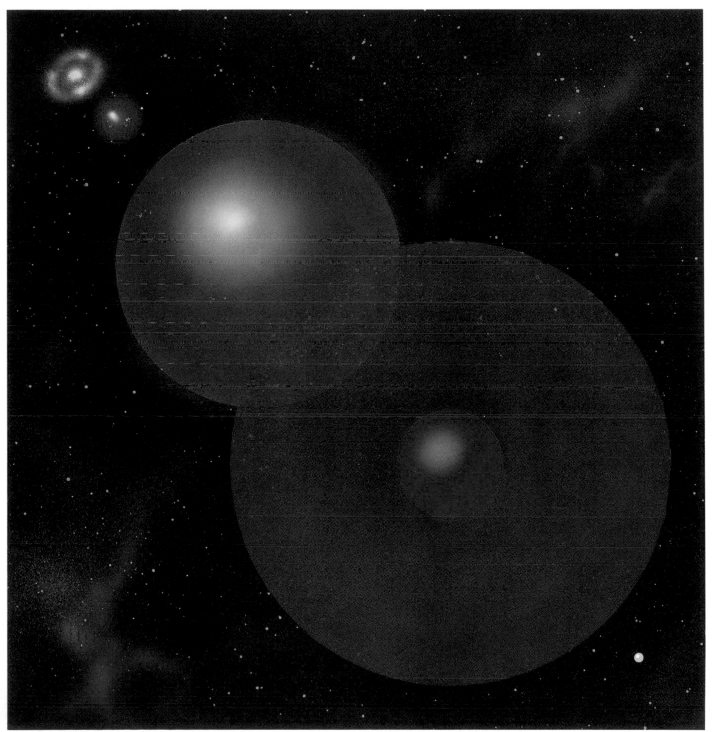

How do stars die?

Many stars spend most of their old age as red giants. Their nuclei are made up of very hot and compressed helium. When the temperature in the center of these stars reaches 200 million degrees, the helium nuclei begin to react.

These new nuclear reactions bring about heavier elements of carbon, nitrogen, and oxygen. The energy produced by these reactions momentarily stops the contraction in the star.

The wrapping of the star is so swollen that the star begins to lose its outer layers, releasing a hydrogen gas bubble. These bubbles are known as **planetary nebulas**, because when seen through a small telescope they appear in the shape of a disc, somewhat similar to a planet.

One of the most spectacular examples of a planetary nebula is the Ring Nebula in the constellation Lyra. The gas bubble appears as a ring because only its edges are visible.

In the center of a planetary nebula there is always a blue-white star. This is the old nucleus of a very compressed and hot red giant which has become exposed after losing its wrapping. Such stars are called **white dwarfs**. They are made up of ice, carbon, and oxygen. They have approximately the same amount of matter as the Sun, but are only as big as the Earth. They have a very high density, thousands of times that of water.

The Sun, and all other stars with similar masses, will end their lives as white dwarfs. They are inert stars that will not evolve further. They start to cool over a period of billions of years, until they become dark dwarfs.

Below: The Ring Nebula in Lyra, the most famous of the planetary nebulas. It is fairly easy to see with a telescope.

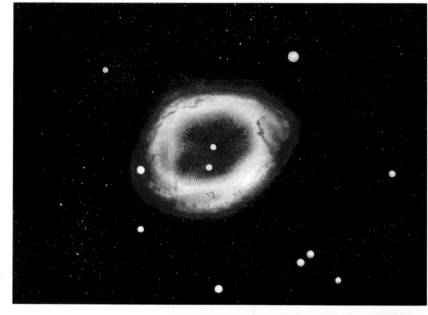

Right: Stars with a mass similar to the Sun end their lives as white dwarfs after losing their wrapping. The density of a white dwarf is very high and it starts to cool very slowly, becoming darker and darker.

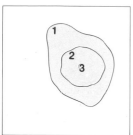

Below: The Helix Nebula is a spectacular example of a planetary nebula. An old star has released a reddish hydrogen gas bubble ①, which can be seen in the form of a ring, with spiral branches. The nebula appears to be empty inside ② because only the edges of the gas bubble can be seen. The hot, dense nucleus of the star is exposed by the expulsion of the gas bubble and appears as a blue star ③ in the geometric center of the nebula.

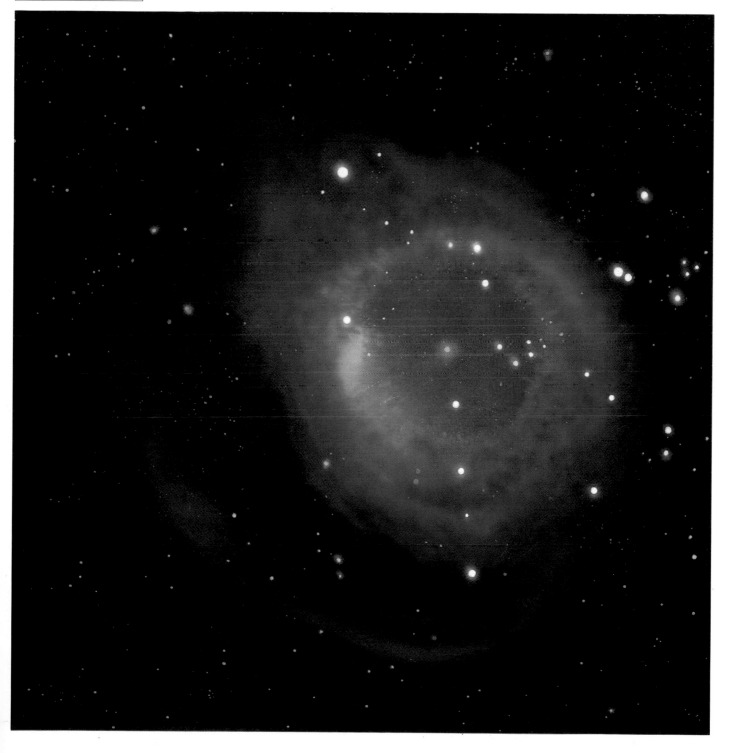

Supernovas, the great fireworks

Not all stars end their lives as quietly as the white dwarfs. Massive stars, with much more matter than the Sun, continue a more complex evolution and finish their existence in a far more spectacular way.

The nucleus of these stars is so compressed and hot that more nuclear reactions can occur. When such a star has used up all of its hydrogen, the nucleus becomes compressed and heats up until the carbon reacts bringing about heavier elements. When the carbon has run out, a similar process begins.

These different phases happen quickly, because the new nuclear reactions produce less energy each time. Toward the end, the star begins to acquire a structure of layers, with the nucleus being made up of iron.

When it is no longer possible to obtain more energy from the iron, the star's center collapses in on itself and the whole star explodes in one great, unimaginable bang.

This explosion can produce a glow of more than one hundred million Suns. We call such an explosion a *supernova*.

Most of the star's matter disperses into space. The explosion produces a rapidly expanding nebula. The Crab nebula in the constellation Taurus is the remains of a supernova that Chinese astronomers saw in 1054.

Below: These filaments are the remains of a supernova explosion that happened more than 10,000 years ago in the constellation Vela, in the southern hemisphere.

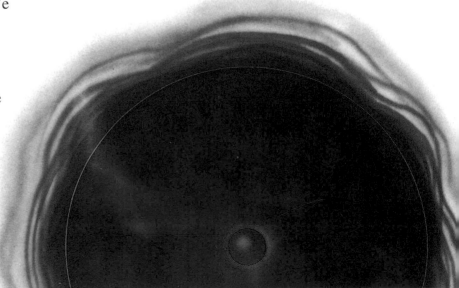

Below: A star just before it explodes as a supernova. It is formed of successive layers of lighter elements: iron in the center, then silicon, magnesium, sulphur, oxygen, neon, carbon, helium, and finally, a hydrogen wrapping. Nuclear reactions that take place between each pair of layers transform one element into another.

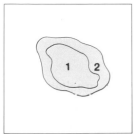

Below: The Crab nebula in the constellation Taurus. It is the remains of a supernova explosion observed in 1054 by Chinese astronomers. A large star exploded ①, hurling part of its matter into space. The nebula's filaments ② are expanding at a great speed through the interstellar medium. Recently in 1987 a relatively close supernova, in the Great Magellanic Cloud, was studied for the first time.

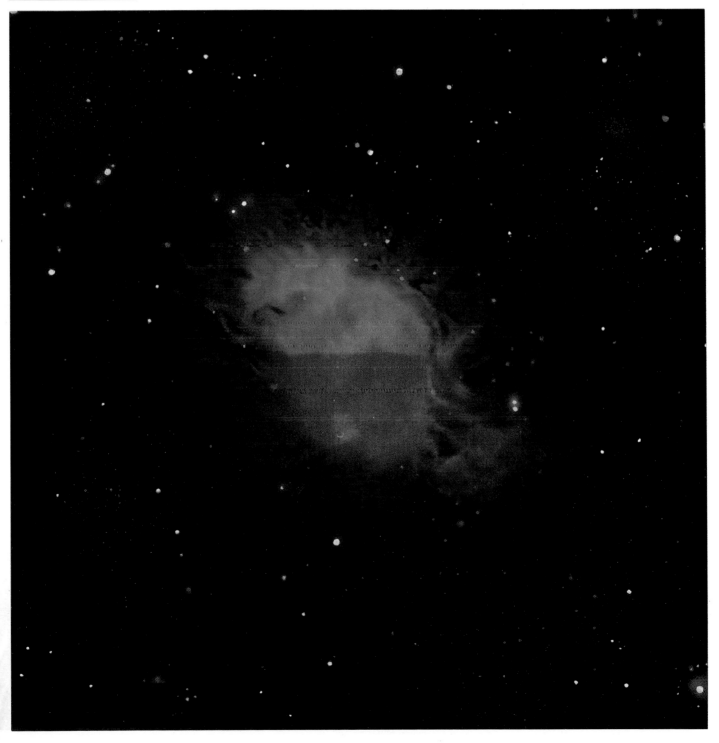

Pulsars, the space beacons

When a supernova explodes, most of the star is destroyed. However, the star's nucleus can survive the explosion. What remains after the explosion is so compressed that it is like an enormous nucleus of an atom. It is called a **neutron star**, since it is primarily made up of neutrons. A teaspoon of this matter would weigh more than a million tons. A neutron star has about the same amount of matter as the Sun, but its diameter measures only about 6 miles (10 km).

Neutron stars do not give off visible light, but they transmit radio waves (another form of electromagnetic radiation, on a wavelength much longer than light). These stars spin very fast on their own, emitting a beam of radiation that spins along with the star, exactly as a lighthouse's lamp does. Each time the beam points to the Earth, we receive a pulse of radiation. This is what is known as a **pulsar**.

Pulsars were first discovered by chance in 1967 by two British radio astronomers. At that time the existence of neutron stars was only a theory. Today we know of hundreds of pulsars in our galaxy, and every year more are discovered. Astronomers hope one day to discover the pulsar that was probably formed after the 1987 supernova explosion in the Great Magellanic Cloud.

The pulsations from pulsars are normally repeated in periods of less than a second. As a pulsar ages, its speed of rotation slows and the pulsations become less frequent. The youngest known pulsar is in the center of the Crab nebula, which is all that remains of the star that exploded in 1054. The Crab's pulsar has a period of 0.033 second, which means that the neutron star rotates 30 times per second. Recently faster pulsars have been discovered, which reach speeds of 500 rotations per second.

Below: In this sequence (that lasts 0.033 second), we can see how the Crab's pulsar regularly flashes on and off. The pulsar is the variable point that appears in the lower part of the image, below and to the right of the brightest star. The flashing on and off repeats 30 times per second.

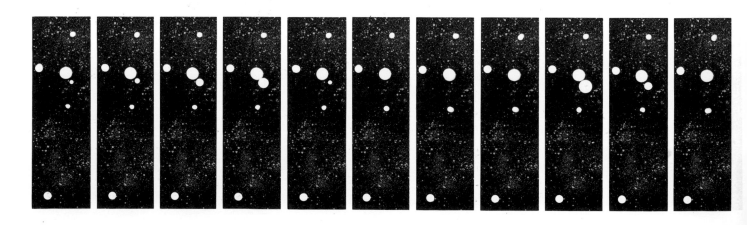

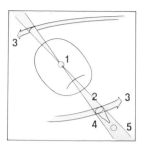

Below: A pulsar is a neutron star ①, which is extremely dense. It is the remains of the nucleus of an exploded star. Neutron stars have a very intense magnetic field ② and they spin very fast ③ on their axis. While spinning, they drag along a radiation beam ④, which works like the lamp of a lighthouse. When the beam is pointing toward the Earth ⑤, we see a radiation pulse.

Do black holes exist?

What happens when a star's nucleus contains an enormous quantity of matter? The neutron star's interior cannot support its own weight so it begins to compress into itself and collapses even further.

But, unlike the other processes in a star's evolution, in this case a surprising thing happens. The star is condemned to totally collapse under its own weight. Its diameter begins to reduce at the same time that its density increases. There is nothing known in nature that is capable of opposing such an intense gravitational force.

How does this process end? Surprisingly, it can be said that it never ends. When the force of gravity is very intense, the effects predicted by the theory of relativity become important, particularly the shrinking of time. We see that the process continuously becomes slower, in such a way that we can never see it end. There are other curious effects that have to do with this theory. At a certain point, gravity is so intense that even light cannot escape from the star in contraction. This is a **black hole**.

Although black holes have never been observed, it is believed that they exist. If in the case of a binary star system, where two stars are close together, one of the objects is a black hole and the other is a giant, a part of the giant's matter will be trapped by the black hole. The matter will begin falling toward the black hole and will heat up considerably and emit X rays.

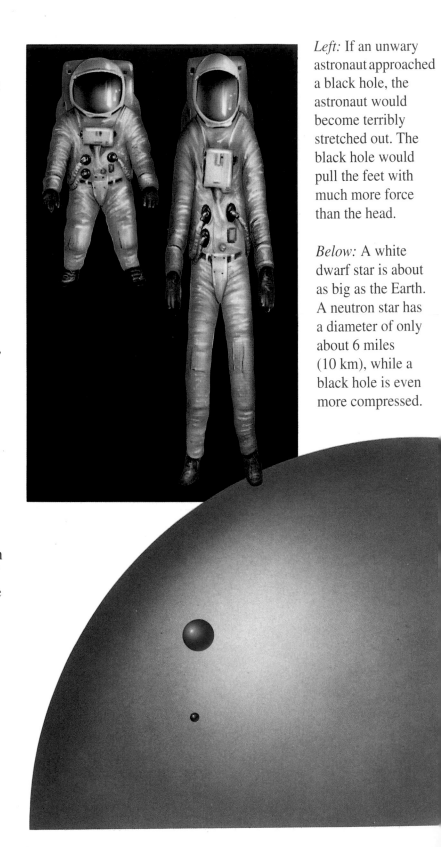

Left: If an unwary astronaut approached a black hole, the astronaut would become terribly stretched out. The black hole would pull the feet with much more force than the head.

Below: A white dwarf star is about as big as the Earth. A neutron star has a diameter of only about 6 miles (10 km), while a black hole is even more compressed.

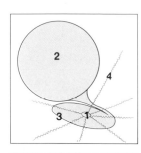

Below: It is suspected that there is a black hole in Cygnus X-1 ①. Cygnus X-1 is a binary star system in which one of the stars is blue ② and its companion, probably a black hole, is a very dense object containing a great mass. The blue star's matter is wrenched by this dense object and forms a disc around it ③. This matter heats up to a very high temperature while falling into the dense object, and emits radiation in the form of X rays ④.

The origin of the elements

There are about a hundred chemical elements in nature, which can be found in an isolated form or as part of the atmosphere, sea, or in the Earth's crust. Nitrogen can be found in the atmosphere, oxygen in seawater, silicon in rocks, and carbon in living beings.

All existing chemical elements, except hydrogen and helium, originated from inside stars. All the new elements were launched into space through the explosion of supernovas. Interstellar matter is enriched by these new chemicals. After a certain period of time, new stars are formed from interstellar material that has already been enriched by elements more complex than helium. Such matter eventually becomes part of the planets that are formed by a star.

The origin of all Earth's atoms that are not hydrogen or helium is the stars, even the atoms of living beings, including ourselves. The matter that forms our bodies originated from the center of a star!

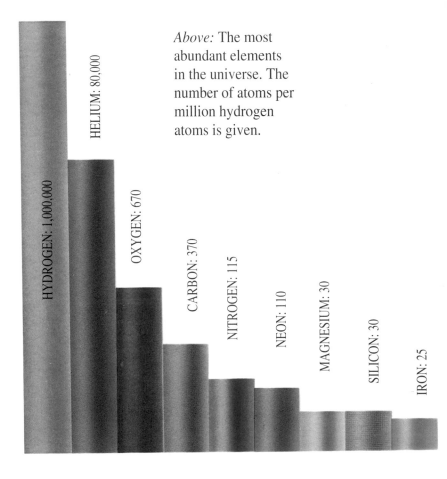

HYDROGEN: 1,000,000

HELIUM: 80,000

OXYGEN: 670

CARBON: 370

NITROGEN: 115

NEON: 110

MAGNESIUM: 30

SILICON: 30

IRON: 25

Above: The most abundant elements in the universe. The number of atoms per million hydrogen atoms is given.

Below: The hydrogen atoms are formed by a proton and an electron. The atoms of helium have a nucleus containing two protons and two neutrons, surrounded by two electrons. Carbon has six protons and six neutrons in its nucleus.

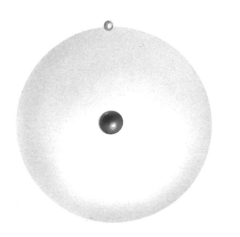

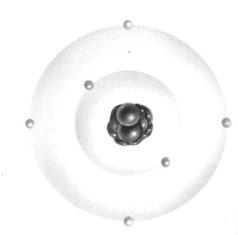

Below: There are about a hundred different chemical elements on Earth. The atoms of the various elements are distinguished by the number of protons in the nucleus, which coincides with the number of electrons in the atom's shell. All elements, except hydrogen and helium, originated from the center of a dense star. When the star explodes as a supernova, as you can see in this illustration, these elements are sent off into space. After some time, they become new stars and planets that are formed from this interstellar material.

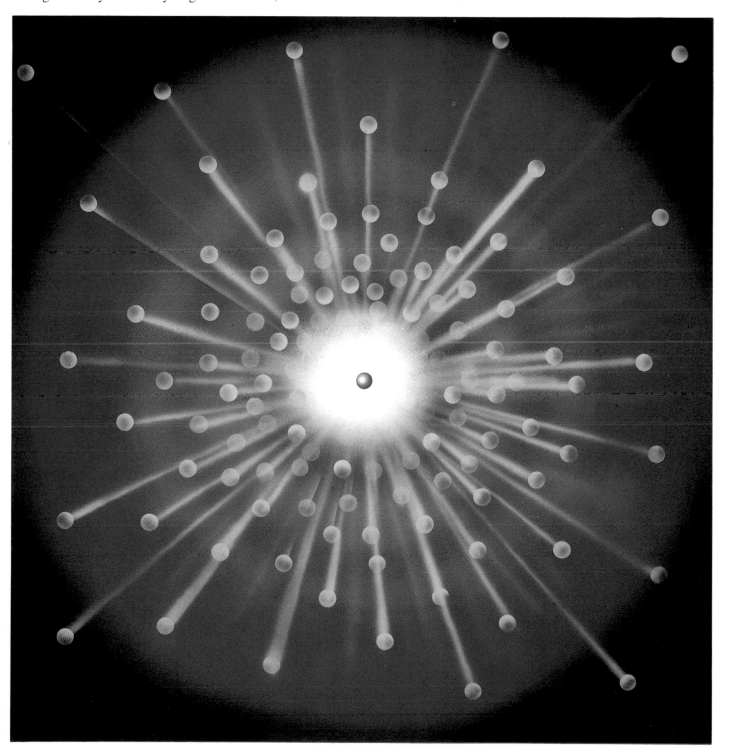

Activity. How many stars are there?

To look at the night sky, we have to choose a place far from the city or town lights, and wait for a clear night, without clouds or fog.

Once our eyes become adapted to the dark, we can observe this great spectacle. Although it is no surprise, it is always breathtaking. There are so many stars, it seems as if they could fall on our heads at any moment.

If the question has any meaning, how many stars are there? A better way to put the question might be: How many stars can we see with our eyes? All the stars we can see belong to our galaxy, the Milky Way galaxy, which contains about 100 billion stars. But even with the biggest telescopes we can see only a small number of them, those that are closest to the Sun. By looking with the naked eye, we can see only the brightest stars, up to the sixth magnitude. In all, that would make a few thousand, about 6,000 if conditions are really excellent.

Counting stars with the naked eye seems to be an impossible job. But it can be done in a simpler way that is a lot of fun. Cut a hole with a diameter of about 5 inches (12 cm) in a piece of

Below: In order to do this activity you will need a piece of cardboard, a compass, a pair of scissors, and a piece of string. Use the compass to draw a circle with a diameter of about 5 inches (12 cm) on the cardboard. Then use the scissors to cut it out.

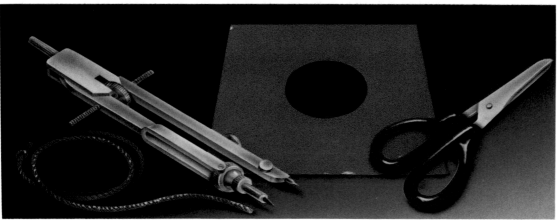

cardboard. Tie a string to the cardboard and make a knot about 12 inches (30 cm) from the card. If you hold the card so that the string is straight and perpendicular to your face, with the knot near your eye, you will see about 1% of the celestial sphere through the hole.

Point the hole toward the sky and count the stars you see though it. Do the same in a total of ten different directions. Add up the number of stars you have counted in each direction and multiply the sum by ten. The answer will be the number of visible stars in the whole sky.

Below: You have to look at the sky through the hole in the cardboard in ten different directions.

Count the number of stars you see through the hole and multiply your answer by 10.

Glossary

Black hole: A very dense object that is thought to be formed from the very high masses of dying stars. The black hole's intense gravitation would be strong enough to even retain light.

Bright nebula: Interstellar dust that is visible near a bright or hot star.

Dark nebula: An interstellar dust cloud that covers the stars behind it.

Fusion: A nuclear reaction in which two or more nuclei come together to create a heavier nucleus. For example, the fusion of four hydrogen nuclei in stars makes way for a helium nucleus from which an enormous quantity of energy is emitted.

Globular cluster: A cluster of stars in the form of a sphere. They are made up of hundreds of thousands to millions of stars.

Interstellar matter: Hydrogen gas and dust that exists in the galaxy between stars.

Light-year: Distance that light travels in one year, equivalent to about 6 trillion miles (10 trillion km).

Neutron star: An extremely dense star, formed by neutrons. This is the final stage of stars with a high mass. Neutron stars are observed as pulsars.

Planetary nebula: A gas bubble expelled by an old star.

Protostar: A star in formation. The protostar's matter contracts due to the effect of its own gravitational pull.

Pulsar: A neutron star that emits high levels of radiation. Since the star rotates very fast on its axis, we perceive the radiation in regular pulses.

Pulsating star: An unstable star whose size and temperature changes rhythmically. As a result, its brightness also varies.

Red giant: An evolutionary stage of a star. It is the moment when the hydrogen in its center runs out. The star swells and cools and becomes red in color.

Star cluster: A group of stars that are close together in space, and were formed at the same time.

Variable star: An unstable star whose brightness varies with its temperature, normally in a periodic manner.

White dwarf: A small high density star. Our Sun will end up as a white dwarf.

Index

Author: Robert Estalella
Illustrator: Marcel Socías

All inquiries should be addressed to:
Barron's Educational Series, Inc.
250 Wireless Boulevard
Hauppauge, New York 11788

Library of Congress Catalog Card No. 93–18077
International Standard Book No. 0-8120-1738-2 (P)
0-8120-6371-6 (H)

Library of Congress Cataloging-in-Publication Data
Available on request.

PRINTED IN SPAIN
3456   987654321